Towns and Cities

Towns and Cities

HERON
BOOKS

Published by
Heron Books, Inc.
20950 SW Rock Creek Road
Sheridan, OR 97378

heronbooks.com

Special thanks to all the teachers and students who
provided feedback instrumental to this edition.

20 December 2022

At Heron Books, we think learning should be engaging and fun. It should be hands-on and allow students to move at their own pace.

To facilitate this we have created a learning guide that will help any student progress through this book, chapter by chapter, with confidence and interest.

Get learning guides at
heronbooks.com/learningguides.

For teacher resources,
such as a final exam, email
teacherresources@heronbooks.com.

We would love to hear from you!
Email us at *feedback@heronbooks.com.*

IN THIS BOOK

CHAPTER 1

Places People Live

Some people live in homes away from everyone else, maybe on a farm or just by themselves out in the country.

Most people live in houses next to other people. Towns and cities are places where people live near each other. Cities are very big, and have lots and lots of people. Towns don't have as many people.

TOWNS

Towns can be very small. A small town might have just a few streets, and just a few stores and shops. People often have to go to a bigger town or city to get all the things they need.

There are usually fields and trees around a small town. People often like small towns because they are quiet. A small town might have a few hundred people or even less.

Bigger towns might have thousands of people, and more houses, stores and shops. You can get food and clothes, and almost everything you need in a town, but you still might need to go to a bigger place, like a city. There is more happening in bigger towns, so they are not as quiet as small towns.

CITIES

This is a city.

A city is a much bigger than a town. Towns grow up and become cities when lots of people, and lots of stores and shops move there.

There may be hundreds of thousands or even millions of people living in a city! In a city, there are always lots of places where people buy and sell things, or make things, or do work for other people.

In some cities, people make cars or computers or dishes or toys. These things are sold to people in other cities and other countries too. Some cities make clothes. Some cities make metal.

There is a lot going on in a city. It is more crowded and noisier than a town.

PLACES PEOPLE LIVE

In the United States, more people live in larger towns and cities. People live there because they can find jobs more easily than in the country or small towns.

Sometimes people like to live in the country or a town, and work in a city. Then they have to drive a long way to work, or take a train or a bus.

The country, towns and cities all can be good places to live. It depends on what you like.

CHAPTER 2

Special Jobs in Towns and Cities

Most people live together in towns and cities.

There are many special jobs that have to be done for a town or city to work well. The people who do these special jobs work for the town or city. They "serve" the people who live in the town or city. **Serve** means to work for and to help a person or group.

Both towns and cities have most of these jobs, but from now on we will talk about cities.

CITY GOVERNMENT

The first special job to talk about is the city government. The **city government** is the group of people who are in charge of the city.

The people in the city government work in a building called **city hall**.

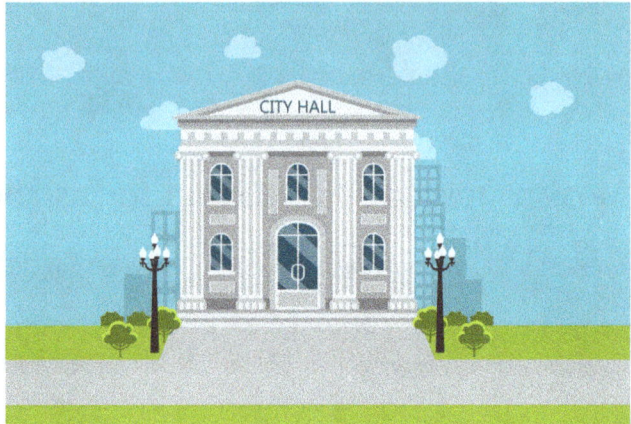

The **mayor** is the leader of the city government. Other people in the city government work for the mayor.

The people in the city government make sure the streets get fixed, and that parks are taken care of. They make sure that all the special jobs of the people who work for the city get done.

They also make sure the city has enough money to do the things it needs to do. One of the things they need money for is to pay people who work for the city.

City halls usually have big meeting rooms. The city government meets in a big meeting room and talks about how to run the city. Many people from the city come to the meetings.

The city government serves the people by keeping the city running smoothly.

CHAPTER 3

Firefighters

One of the special jobs in a city is firefighter. A **firefighter** is a person who puts out fires in the city.

When there is a fire in a house or building, they go there as fast as they can in their fire trucks. They have big water hoses on their trucks that they attach to a fire plug near the fire. Fire plugs are like big faucets attached to the city water pipes.

Firefighters keep their fire trucks at the fire station. Often some of the firefighters even live at the fire station part of the time. This is so, if a fire starts, they can get in their trucks right away.

Firefighters serve the people by keeping the city safe from fire.

CHAPTER 4

Police Officers

Another special job is police officer. A **police officer** is a person who makes sure people follow the law. When someone is in trouble, they call the police to come and help them.

Police officers walk or drive around the city to notice if anything is wrong. Sometimes they even ride horses! They help keep cars and trucks moving on crowded streets, and help when people have car accidents.

Police officers work at the police station.

Police officers serve the people by keeping the city safe.

CHAPTER 5

Judges

A judge is another special job in a city. **Judges** decide what is the right thing to do when a law is broken or when people have an important disagreement. The judge also settles arguments.

Judges work in a large room called a courtroom.

Sometimes the courtroom is in city hall. Other times it is in its own building call the **courthouse**.

Suppose Jack has broken the law. Let's say he threw trash on the ground and the police officer saw him.

In the courtroom, the policeman tells the judge what Jack did.

Jack tells the judge his side of the story.

People in the courtroom listen.

The judge decides what should be done. Sometimes other people help the judge decide.

Perhaps the judge decides Jack must pick up the trash and Jack must pay $25 for throwing trash on the ground.

Judges serve the people in the city by making fair decisions about what should be done when a law is broken or when people have important disagreements.

CHAPTER 6

Garbage Collectors

Another special job in a city is garbage or trash collector. A **garbage collector** is a person who picks up the trash and garbage in the city.

Garbage collectors put the garbage from the houses and buildings into their trucks.

They take the garbage to a **landfill**. This is a place close to the city where all the garbage can be put safely. A giant hole is dug with a big tractor, or even bigger machines. The garbage is dumped and covered with earth (dirt).

The hole is filled up with layers of garbage and earth.

When the whole landfill is filled, it is usually planted with trees and grass, and made into a park.

Just think how dirty the city would be if there weren't garbage collectors doing their jobs!

Garbage collectors serve the people by keeping trash and garbage from piling up in the city.

CHAPTER 7

City Drivers

Cities often have buses and trains for people to use to get from one place to another in the city. Sometimes the trains go through tunnels underground. Then they are called subways. Buses and trains need drivers.

A **city driver** is a person who drives the city buses and trains.

City drivers serve the people by driving them around the city.

CHAPTER 8

Utility Workers

Houses need electricity, water, gas for stoves, and a place for dirty water from sinks and toilets to go. These things are called **utilities**.

stove

sink

lamp

The people who make sure we have these things are called **utility workers**.

Utility workers put pipes in the ground to bring water and gas to all the houses, and different pipes to take dirty water away.

They put up poles and wires to bring electricity.

Another place utility workers work is called a sewage plant. The dirty water that drains from a sink or toilet is called waste water or **sewage**. It goes to a **sewage plant** where it gets cleaned up. (The word **plant** here means a large place or building where there are machines that make something, or do some kind of work.)

Utility workers serve the people by making sure they have electricity, gas, water and a place for dirty water to go.

CHAPTER 9

Places to Serve People

There are many places in a city that serve the people. Let's talk about a few of them.

LIBRARY

A **library** is a place that has lots of books that it will loan to you. You can pick out a book to take home and read. Then you can bring it back and pick another one.

Cities usually have more than one library. Most libraries have a part for grown-ups and a part for children. Schools also have libraries.

A **librarian** is a person who takes care of a library.

SCHOOL

A **school** is a place where you can learn.

Cities usually have lots of schools. There are many different kinds of schools. They can be big or small.

Teachers work at schools, and help you learn many things.

POST OFFICE

A **post office** is a place that makes sure mail goes where it is supposed to go.

When you put a letter in a mailbox, it gets picked up and taken to the post office. The person who picks up and delivers the mail is called a **letter carrier.**

People in the post office sort all the mail to get it ready to go to the place it's supposed to go.

Then a letter carrier picks it up and takes it to the mailbox at that address.

HOSPITAL

A **hospital** is a big place where people can go if they are sick or hurt. Doctors and nurses work there, and they can help people get better. If they need to, people can stay overnight at hospitals while they get better.

Most cities have at least one hospital.

CHAPTER 10

Houses and Apartments

There are many kinds of buildings in towns and cities, and they are used for lots of things.

One important kind of building people need is a place to live.

Some people live in houses. **Houses** are buildings for people to live in that are separate from other buildings.

houses

Sometimes many people live in one larger building. A family usually has a group of rooms that is separate from the rooms other families live in. The group of rooms is called an **apartment**, because it is "apart" from the other rooms.

An **apartment building** can have a lot of apartments and many families can have apartments in one building. Apartments can be big or small. Some apartments are as big as big houses, but most apartments are smaller than a house.

apartment

CHAPTER 11

Warehouses, Stores and Shops

Warehouses, stores and shops all have to do with selling things to people in the city.

A **warehouse** is a big building that is used to store things to sell. When you **store** something, you put it in a safe place until you need it. **Ware** means "something to sell." Warehouses keep things for stores until stores need more things to sell. Then trucks take the things to the stores.

Sometimes people sell things at warehouses. But mostly things are just stored there.

A **store** is a building where things are stored *and* sold.

Lots of things are sold in stores.

A **shop** is a small store. A shop may not have so much to sell and it usually doesn't have room to store lots and lots of things.

There are stores that sell just about anything that people need. The reason we have stores is that people need things. Then somebody thinks, "Hey, I could make money by getting those things and selling them."

Everybody needs clothes, so some people have clothing stores.

Of course, everyone needs food! For food, there are grocery stores.

Groceries are foods and other things for the house that you can buy. A **grocery store** sells mainly food and some other things for the house. Grocery stores come in many sizes. Sometimes you can buy food in a small shop.

Some grocery stores are medium-sized and some are very big. The very big ones are often called **supermarkets**.

A **gas station** is a different kind of store that sells gasoline for your car. Sometimes it will also sell snacks and things to drink.

Another kind of store is a hardware store. A **hardware store** sells things you can use to build and to repair things. Remember, **ware** means "something to sell," so hardware means things to sell that are hard. Actually not *everything* in a hardware store is hard, but many things are.

Hardware store

You can find locks,

tools,

knives, pots, spoons,

and other things.

Sometimes large stores have different parts that sell different kinds of things. These parts of the store are called **departments**. A **department store** is a store that has many of these departments. Each department sells something different.

A **hobby** is something you like to do for fun. **Hobby shops** sell games, paints, model airplanes, and many other things.

A **restaurant** is a kind of store where you can buy meals. There are lots of different kinds of restaurants.

A **shopping center** is a group of buildings together that has many stores, shops and offices. The shopping center has a big parking lot for cars to park while the people are there. You can find almost everything you want to buy at a shopping center.

CHAPTER 12

Office Buildings

An **office building** is a building that has many rooms where people can work. The rooms are called **offices**.

There are usually lots of office buildings in cities. In this picture, many of the tall buildings are office buildings.

Sometimes the people who own or run big stores have offices in office buildings. Although they work in the office building, what they do there is make sure the store runs correctly. The office people keep track of what happens in the store and sometimes tell the store people what to do.

People in this office building might run these stores:

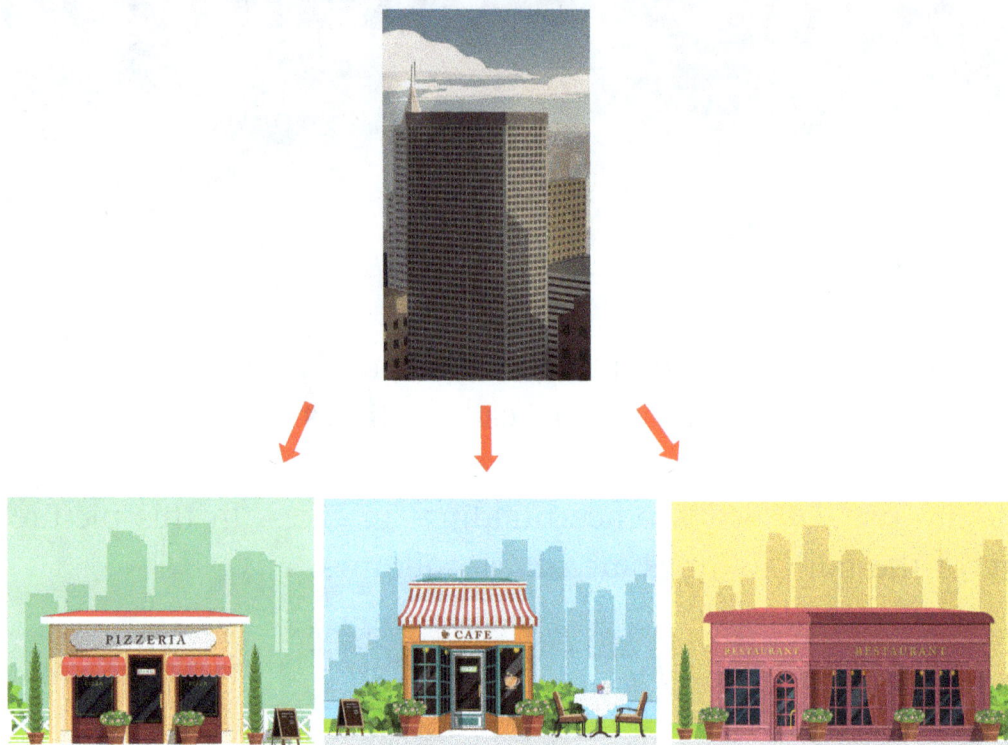

People who work in office buildings usually have desks in their offices. They do things like have meetings, call people on phones, and work at computers

CHAPTER 13

Buildings for Services

Buildings are also used to give you services. A **service** is something someone does for other people that they want done.

We know that a shop is a small store. But people also use the word **shop** for some buildings where people do services.

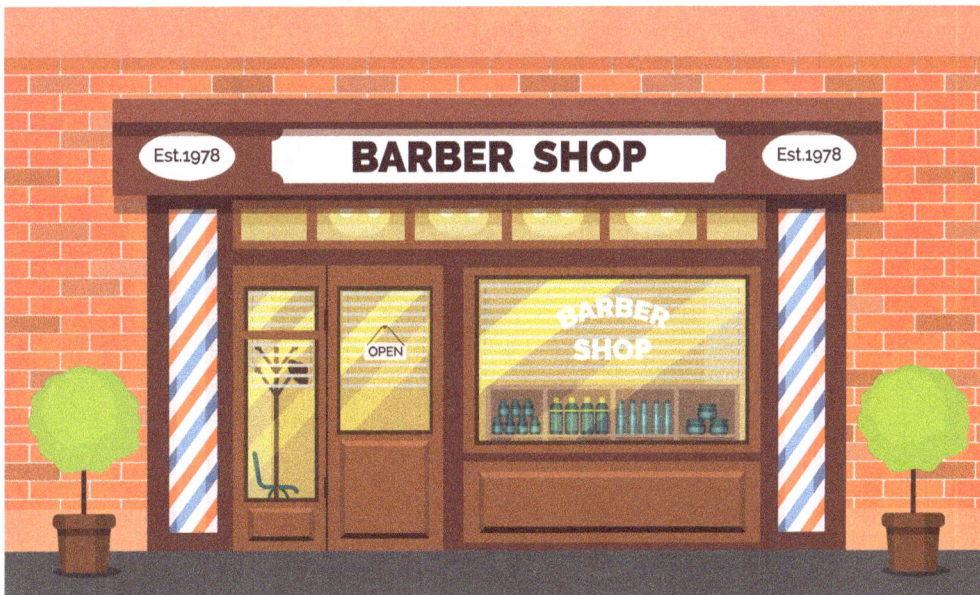

The barber cuts your hair at a barber shop. The haircut is a service.

You can take things that need to be fixed to a **repair shop**. Fixing your TV is a service.

The person at an auto repair shop can fix your car. An auto repair shop is also called a **garage**. Fixing your car is a service.

A **doctor's office** is the place a doctor usually works. You can go to the doctor's office, and the doctor will help you get well or stay healthy. Helping you be healthy is a service.

doctor's office

A **bank** can keep your money for you. Keeping your money is a service.

There are many services you can get in a city. Now you know a few of them!

CHAPTER 14

Factories

A **factory** is a big building where things are made. Some factories have many buildings.

Factories make all sorts of different things that are sold in stores. The things the factory makes are often loaded on trucks to go to warehouses or stores.

One factory might make toys, another might make desks, another one might make skateboards. Big factories make cars, trains, airplanes and things like that.

CHAPTER 15

The Parts of a City

Cities usually have different parts.

Where you live is called your home, of course. Another word that is used for this is **residence**. Your house or your apartment is a residence. The part of a city made up mostly of houses and apartments is called **residential**.

residential area

There can be a few stores, shops and offices in a residential area, but it is mainly just residences.

The place where people work to make money is called a business. Stores, shops and offices are businesses. If a part of a city is made up almost entirely of stores and shops and offices, it is called a **business area**. Sometimes when an area has mostly just stores and shops, it can be called a **shopping area**.

There can be a few houses and apartments in a business or shopping area, but it is mostly businesses.

Often the place where most of the businesses are is in the middle of the city. Then the area is called **downtown**.

Some cities have factories close together in the same part of the city. Then this part of the city would be called the **factory area**.

You can live in the residential area. You can work in the business or factory area. Where can you play in a city? You can play in a **park**. A park is a piece of land for fun and play.

It can be wild.

It can be grassy.

It can have swings and playground equipment.

It can have other things, like a zoo.

How do you go from one part of the city to another part of the city? You can use a sidewalk or a street.

If you want to go from one city or town to another, you can use a large street called a **highway**.

Some highways are made so you don't have to stop for other cars, or even when you drive through a city. This kind of highway is called a **freeway**. You can drive the fastest on a freeway.

CHAPTER 16

Living in Towns and Cities

Most people like to live around other people. Some people like to live around a *lot* of other people. This is why we have towns and cities.

In the towns and cities, people build houses and apartment buildings to live in.

When people live around other people, they need a city government to make sure special jobs in the city are done, and the city runs smoothly.

The city government makes sure the city has utilities like electricity and water and a sewage plant for dirty water.

People want to buy things and get services. So people start businesses to provide these things.

People build stores and factories and warehouses. People build restaurants and office buildings.

People build libraries, parks and schools. They build highways to drive to other cities.

Towns can start very small, and then grow and grow into a big city. Some towns stay small.

Now you know a lot about towns and cities. Find out more interesting things by asking questions, and visiting places in your town or city!